HOW'S YOUR HEALTH?

Asthma

Angela Royston

W
FRANKLIN WATTS
LONDON • SYDNEY

First published in 2006 by
Franklin Watts
338 Euston Road
London NW1 3BH

Franklin Watts Australia
Hachette Children's Books
Level 17/207 Kent Street
Sydney NSW 2000

Copyright © Franklin Watts 2006

Produced by Calcium, New Brook House, 385 Alfreton Road, Nottingham, NG7 5LR

Editor: Sarah Eason
Design: Paul Myerscough
Illustration: Annie Boberg and Geoff Ward
Picture research: Sarah Jameson
Consultant: Dr Stephen Earwicker

Acknowledgements:
The publisher would like to thank the following for permission to reproduce photographs:
Alamy p.8, p.26, p.27; CMSP p.11; Istockphoto p.16, p.20; OSF p.18; Getty p.19; Corbis
p.14, p.15; Chris Fairclough Photography p.6, p.12, p.13, p.17, p.21, p.22, p.23, p.24, p.25;
Inmagine p.7.

A CIP catalogue record for this book is available from the British Library.

Dewey Decimal Classification Number: 616.2'38

ISBN-10: 0 7496 6673 0
ISBN-13: 978 0 7496 6673 6

Printed in China

Contents

What is asthma?

Asthma makes it difficult for a person to **breathe**.

People with asthma often cough. They also make a **wheezing** sound when they breathe. This is because it is difficult for air to move into and out of their **lungs**.

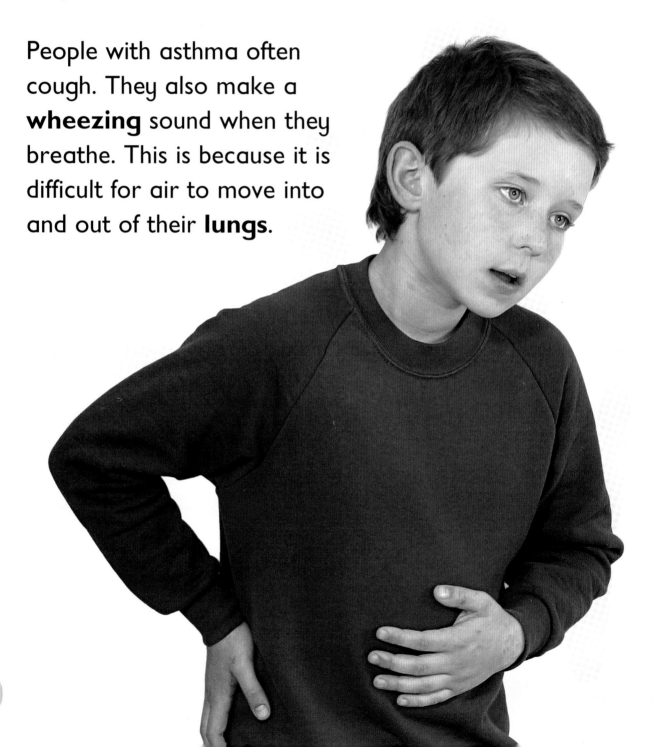

Our bodies can only work well when we breathe properly. People with asthma find it difficult to breathe sometimes, which can make them ill. However, many people who have asthma breathe normally most of the time. They can work, play and have fun just like everyone else.

Why is it difficult to breathe with asthma?

Asthma makes the **airways** in the lungs narrow. This makes it hard for air to pass through them.

When you breathe in, you suck in air through your nose or mouth. The air then passes into your lungs through many tiny tubes, called airw

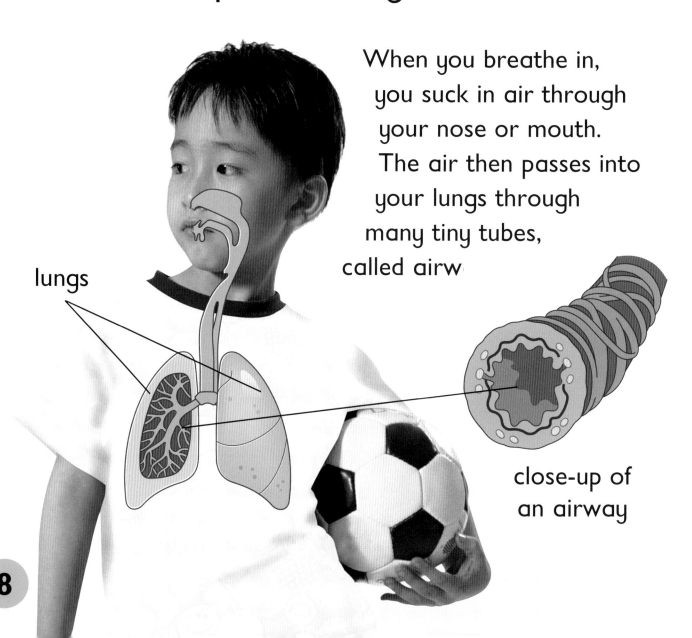

lungs

close-up of an airway

If you have asthma, your airways are always a little swollen. This makes them narrower than other people's airways.

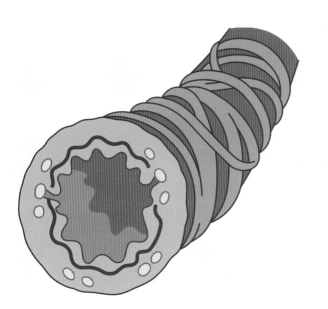

normal airway

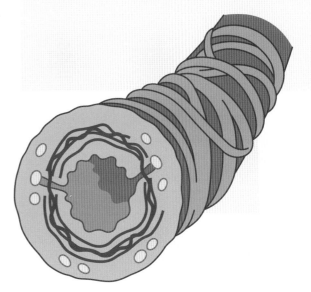

swollen airway

Try this!

1. Pour yourself a drink of water.
2. Use a wide straw to suck up the water.
3. Now use a narrow straw.

Which straw is easier to drink with?

What is an asthma attack?

An **asthma attack** is when a person's asthma gets much worse.

Sometimes a person's airways become tight and fill with **mucus**. This makes them even harder to breathe through. People wheeze more loudly when this happens.

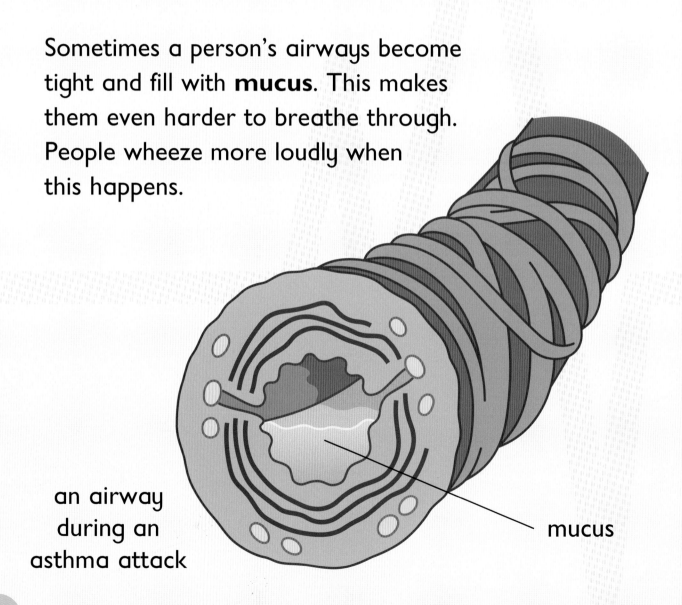

an airway during an asthma attack

mucus

Try this!

1. Pour some water into a glass or mug.
2. Use a straw to suck it up.
3. Empty out the water and pour in some smoothie or other thick liquid. Use the same straw to suck it up.

Which liquid is easier to drink?

Coughing helps to clear mucus out of the airways. Once a person starts coughing, the asthma attack begins to go.

What stops an asthma attack?

An asthma attack stops when the airways relax and become wider so air can pass through them again.

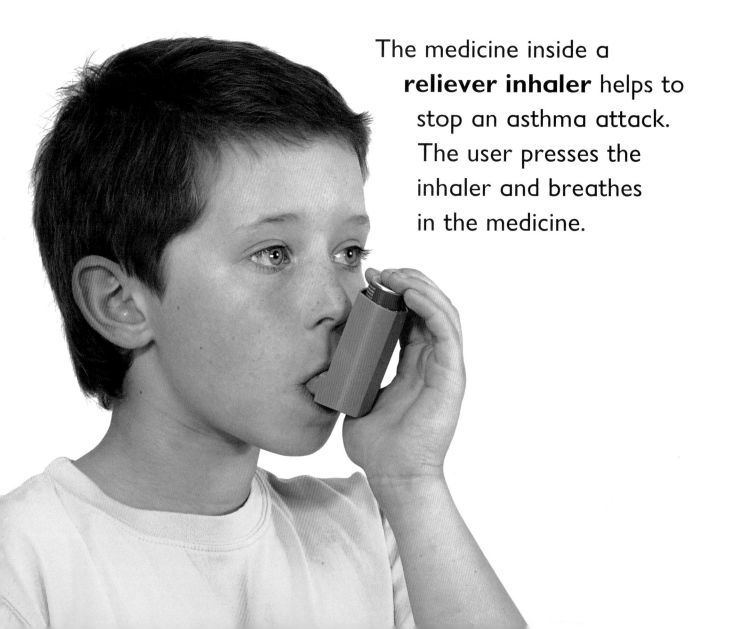

The medicine inside a **reliever inhaler** helps to stop an asthma attack. The user presses the inhaler and breathes in the medicine.

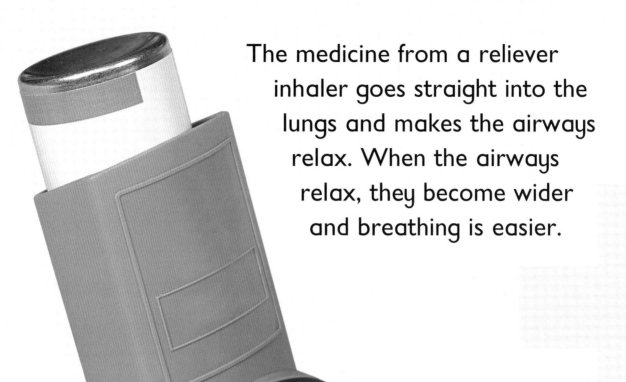

The medicine from a reliever inhaler goes straight into the lungs and makes the airways relax. When the airways relax, they become wider and breathing is easier.

a reliever inhaler

Reliever inhalers

+ A reliever inhaler is usually blue or grey.
+ Breathing in the medicine works more quickly than swallowing it as a pill or liquid.
+ Never use anyone's inhaler or medicine if you do not have asthma.

13

What happens if an asthma attack is bad?

If an asthma attack is very bad, the person may have to go to hospital.

A reliever inhaler may not be enough to stop a bad asthma attack. During a strong attack, people are usually taken to hospital. There they are given a different medicine to help them breathe.

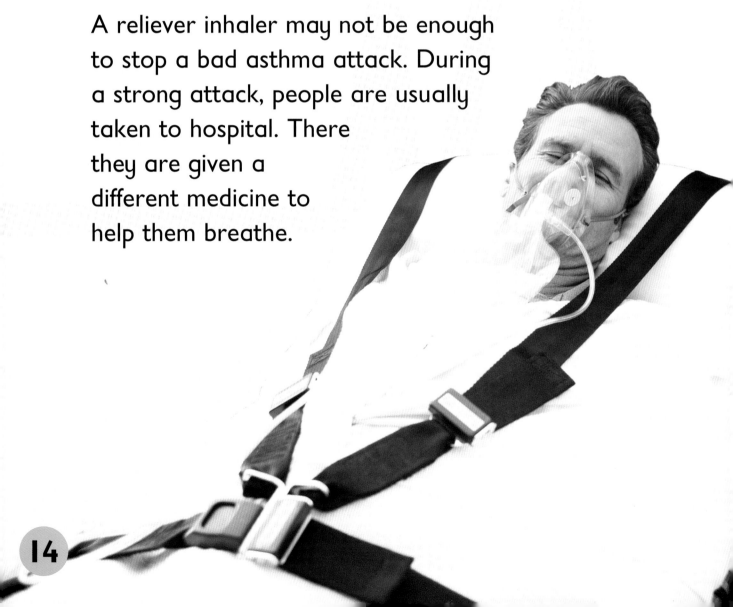

How you can help:

+ If you have asthma, always carry your reliever inhaler.
+ Stay calm.
+ If someone near you has an asthma attack, stay calm. Offer to help them find their inhaler.

An asthma attack passes more quickly if the person stays calm. Being worried or frightened makes the airways tighten more. If someone has an asthma attack it is important to keep them calm.

Can you catch asthma?

You cannot catch asthma from someone who has it.

All sorts of people have asthma. No one knows why some people have it and others don't. People of all ages have asthma.

Asthma often runs in families. People are most likely to have asthma if one of their parents has an **allergy**.

What is an allergy?

An allergy is when your body reacts to something that doesn't affect most other people. An allergy makes you feel ill. Many people with asthma are **allergic** to things they breathe in.

What causes an asthma attack?

Many different things can cause an asthma attack.

When some people breathe in dust or **pollen**, it makes their nose run and their eyes itch. It can also make their asthma worse.

pollen

Things that can cause an asthma attack:

+ The smell of paint, air fresheners, glues, cleaning fluids or **cosmetics**.
+ Fumes from gas stoves and heaters.
+ Dust in mattresses and carpets.
+ Cigarette smoke.
+ Coughing.
+ Cold air.

Some people are allergic to pets.
Pets have fine dust in their fur or feathers,
which makes some people sneeze or
cough. This can cause an asthma attack.

Does worry make asthma worse?

Feeling worried or scared can make asthma worse.

This boy is worried about starting at a new school. He is frightened because everything is strange. This may make his asthma worse.

This boy does not like it when his mother is very angry. It makes his asthma worse.

Why does worry make asthma worse?

When someone with asthma becomes worried their airways get tighter. This makes them narrower, which makes it more difficult to breathe.

What can people do to ease their asthma?

People should try to stay away from things that make their asthma worse.

People who are allergic to dust can use a vacuum cleaner with special **filters**. The filters stop very fine dust travelling through the vacuum and back into the air.

How you can help:

✚ Stay away from things that make your asthma worse.

✚ If pets give someone you know asthma, keep your pet away from them.

Cats and dogs make this girl's asthma worse, so she is careful not to get too close to them.

How else can people help their asthma?

Using a **preventer inhaler** twice a day can stop asthma attacks from happening.

People use a preventer inhaler in the same way that they use a reliever inhaler. They press the inhaler and breathe in. The medicine in a preventer inhaler is different from that in a reliever inhaler.

The medicine in a preventer inhaler makes the airways less swollen. This makes an asthma attack less likely to happen.

a preventer inhaler

Preventer inhalers

A preventer inhaler may be brown, red, white or orange. The medicine inside builds up in the person's body every time it is used. It takes up to two weeks before the medicine is at its strongest.

Does asthma stop people doing things?

Most people with asthma can do the same things as other people.

People sometimes use their reliever inhaler before they play games or exercise. They may also carry the reliever inhaler with them in case they have an asthma attack.

People with asthma can still play sports. Some of the most successful athletes in the world have asthma.

Famous athletes who have asthma:

+ Renn Critchlow – world **kayak** champion.
+ Debbie Meyer – Olympic swimming medalist.
+ Jim Hunter – professional baseball player.
+ Alberto Salazar – **marathon** runner.

Glossary

airway tube in the lungs through which air passes.

allergic to have an allergy.

allergy when the body reacts to something as though it is harmful, although it is harmless to most people.

asthma attack when the airways in someone's lungs tighten so that they find it difficult to breathe.

breathe to take in and let out air through the mouth and nose.

cosmetics creams and make-up that people put on their skin.

filter screen that lets some things through, such as air, but which holds other things back, such as dust or pollen.

kayak small, narrow boat, like a canoe, that holds one or two people.

lung part of the body that breathes in and breathes out air.

marathon very long-distance running race.

mucus thick liquid that is made by the body. Mucus comes out of your nose when it is runny.

pollen fine yellow dust made by flowers, grass and some trees in spring and early summer.

preventer inhaler contains medicine that is breathed in to prevent an asthma attack.

reliever inhaler contains medicine that is breathed in to stop an asthma attack.

wheeze sound that people make when they are finding it difficult to breathe.

Find out more

Lots of facts about asthma: www.airplay.ie

A fun website for children with asthma:
www.asthma-kids.ca

Find out what it is like to have asthma
and how people can cope with it:
www.asthma.org.uk

A site about sport and asthma:
www.getasthmahelp.org/kids_sports.asp

Every effort has been made by the Publisher to ensure that these websites contain no
inappropriate or offensive material. However, because of the nature of the Internet, it is
impossible to guarantee that the contents of these sites will not be altered. We strongly
advise that Internet access is supervised by a responsible adult.

Index